UNDER THE TREE
an Advent resource

PETE TOWNSEND

kevin
mayhew

First published in 2002 by
KEVIN MAYHEW LTD
Buxhall, Stowmarket, Suffolk, IP14 3BW
Email: info@kevinmayhewltd.com

© 2002 Pete Townsend

The right of Pete Townsend to be identified as the author
of this work has been asserted by him in accordance
with the Copyright, Designs and Patents Act, 1988.

The material in this book first appeared in *Café Logos,* Years A, B and C.

9 8 7 6 5 4 3 2 1 0

ISBN 1 84003 939 6
Catalogue No. 1500526

Cover design by Angela Selfe
Edited by Elisabeth Bates
Typesetting by Louise Selfe
Illustrations by David Bill

Printed and bound in Great Britain

Contents

Acknowledgements

Thanks, as ever, to a diverse crowd of people who have, knowingly and unknowingly, given me such precious gifts as friendship, love, hope, laughter, patience and the occasional hankie.

Most of all a large, gift-wrapped parcel of thanks to Liz for being, sort of, there or somewhere useful anyway. A humungous ribbon-covered box of love to Ruth for being around and close by and with me a lot, or at least most of the time. Finally, a glass of cheer to Ed and Jane, Billy and Sharon and lots of other folk with red noses and reindeer antlers.

Introduction

Christmas is amazing! No sooner has one Christmas finished than we're searching through the January sales trying to find the next present for Great-Aunt Agnes. Oh! and while we're there we just happen to come across some Christmas cards at half the marked price and that book of chocolate-cake recipes that would go down a treat with Uncle Joe. A quick shuffle around the shop and we've found presents for all the relatives, the dog, cat and budgie, along with a few pairs of bizarrely patterned socks that will do for anyone we happen to have forgotten. Of course, there's always a couple of unwanted presents that we hope to offload onto some unsuspecting niece or nephew.

The same thing happens every year, but every year we can't wait to see what our presents are going to be (even though we have a sneaking suspicion that the parcel coated in ten rolls of sellotape and a large label with 'Don't open till Christmas' scrawled all over it, bears all the tell-tale signs of Granny's wrapping expertise and the usual gifts of socks, gloves and a jar of pickled gherkins!). The great thing about it all is that it doesn't matter. There is still a thrill in unwrapping the obvious present and mouthing a groan as we hold the socks and pickled gherkins up for everyone to see and we make another groan as Cousin Ted wonders, aloud, about which item will smell the worst after a few days!

It's exciting (not the smelling bit!). We know what it's all about but the whole thing still thrills the socks off us (nice two-tone grey ones with a little blue ship embroidered on them). The odd-shaped, and oddly wrapped, presents provide us with a sense of anticipation and expectancy. Just as some of the presents will cause us to smile, laugh and even frown, so too will *Under the Tree* provide you with a similar mixture of emotions.

Christmas is literally a time to remember Christ and what he was born to accomplish. He himself was the one present that humankind had been waiting for but were unsure of what to make of this rather unconventional gift.

Under the Tree gives us the opportunity to look at what Christmas is all about and 'unwrap' some of the things that God wants us to enjoy. So, take a look under the tree and have fun.

Each of the following units has been divided into six sections with icons for easy recognition:

Christmas list

An introduction to the Bible reading and main theme.

Waking up to Christmas

An idea for activities which may help bring the theme into focus.

Christmas stocking

A link to the teaching, using some ideas for worship.

Unwrapping the presents

The main teaching bit with some ideas and guidelines for sharing.

Christmas crackers

Some more ideas for discussion and thought.

Christmas pudding

Some suggestions for reflection and prayer.

The references to worship songs are only suggestions. You can substitute other material on a similar theme if you prefer. You can either use the worship songs as part of group worship or use the lyrics in discussion. All of the worship suggestions can be found in *The Source*, *The Source 2*, *The Source New Songs*, *Re:source 2000* and *World Wide Worship No. 1*, all of which are published by Kevin Mayhew Ltd.

Expect the unexpected! _____

Matthew 24:36-44: No one knows the day or time

Equipment:
piece of string
sticky tape
paper
pens

As each member of the group arrives, give them a piece of paper and a pen. Ask them to write their name on the paper. As they do this place the piece of string along the length of the room and stick each end down with the tape. Mark one end of the string: 'Dead, buried and that's it' and the other end of the string: 'Journey's end'. Ask the group to consider the question: 'Is death the end of our existence or is there something more?'

After a few moments ask the group to stand somewhere along the string which corresponds with their idea or thoughts of 'life after death'. If any of the group are unsure, which you should stress isn't a problem, then they are to stand somewhere in the middle of the string. If any of the group think there may be an afterlife but aren't certain, then they should stand nearer to 'Journey's end'. And if any of the group think an afterlife is possibly stretching things a bit too far, then they should stand nearer to the 'Dead and buried' end. Once they are all satisfied with their position, then ask them to stick, using the tape, their name onto the string indicating where they stood.

(Allow 10 minutes for this.)

There are few certainties in life and, at times, we even question what we thought we were certain about! Have a look at 'Did you feel the mountains tremble?' (*The Source*, 80; *The British Worship Collection*, 18) or 'I am walking on the way ahead' (*The Australian Worship Collection*, 26).

(Allow 5 minutes for this.)

Remind everyone that the group is supposed to be a non-threatening environment and nobody is to think any less of another person because they may have a different perspective than some other group members.

Read Matthew 24:36-44.

If any of us were to say that we weren't just the teeniest bit interested in what the future holds then they've either got life totally sorted and know how to sort out every global problem (answers on a postcard, please) or they're too busy writing their autobiography to care. Life is unreliable. No matter how we look at life or how much we look at the clock and complain about the monotony of our existence, anything, and everything, can change within a split second.

Lots of people spend money and time trying to predict their future and what it holds for them. The question is, does knowing what is going to happen in a few days', months' or even years' time change the way we think and live now?

Just say, for instance, that someone read your palm and said you were going to win a fortune. So, you go and live according to that prediction and use every bit of credit and hire purchase that you can lay your paws on. And . . . the bills arrive quickly followed by a solicitor's letter suggesting that you'd better pay the money back, with mega-large interest, asap. Alternatively, you might decide that if life is so unpredictable and that it could end quite unexpectedly, then you should live life to the full, right now, this instant or even sooner and ignore everyone in the pursuit of pleasure. Pretty soon you've got no friends, no money and no idea how much more of this pleasure trip you can take.

In reality, most of us don't live as if nothing and no one matter. We have people we care for and hope that they care for us. We try and save some money for the future or have an insurance policy as a protection against the unexpected. We are urged to make the most of our future by putting money into a pension scheme just so that we can enjoy our retirement (that is if we aren't too wasted to enjoy it). But the nagging thoughts still continue, 'Is this it?', 'What are we here for?', 'Have I missed the bus?'

As Jesus chats with his disciples, he tells them that at some point he wants to come back. The disciples must have thought he was barking mad but only Jesus knew that his time on earth was limited and the purpose of his human life was soon to be made painfully obvious. Jesus suggests that people will forget or ignore what he's said and done and live as if they weren't accountable to anyone. But, Jesus reminds them, the 'Son of Man' will return when people least expect it. This isn't used as a threat but as a promise that soon evil will become subject to the authority of Heaven, and that Jesus' return will signal the time when the ravages of evil will be put right.

No one knows when all that Jesus said will actually happen. All we do know is to expect the unexpected!

Give each group member another piece of paper and a pen. Ask them to draw a line across the centre of the page and mark where they stand in relation to Jesus. Do they accept and believe what he said or do they think he was just a wise bloke who got on the wrong side of the authorities? Alternatively they may be somewhere in between the two points of view.

Their thoughts and the piece of paper are private and once they have made their mark on the piece of paper they should fold it up and place it in a pocket or somewhere safe.

(Give the group 5 minutes to do this.)

Ask the group to be still for a few moments and then read the following prayer:

Lord,
    you know
    that whatever we think,
    whatever we say,
    or whatever we do
    has a consequence.
We are not alone
    and we don't live in a void.
There is a world around us
    filled with hurting, crying, worried and frightened people
    who feel as if their life
    has been squashed, crushed, contorted,
    twisted and bruised.
They don't know what the future holds
    and many don't care
    as long as it looks nothing like their today.
While for some of us,
    life seems to pass by
    in a sort of monotonous grey colour
    with no bright bits
    and very few dark bits.
But whatever we think,
    whatever we know, or think we know,
    you've said
    that the only thing we can depend upon
    is you,
    and that really is an unexpected bonus
    considering that we have such
    a fragile grasp
    on life, the universe and everything.

A fruit and nut case?

Matthew 3:1-12: The preaching of John the Baptist

Equipment:
pen
paper
A3 sheet of paper
different images collected from magazines

Distribute pens and paper to the group. Explain that it is often extremely difficult to understand what some people are trying to say or precisely what they mean. For instance, if someone were to say that they were 'Drouthy', would anyone know what they meant? (Drouthy means to be thirsty.) Ask the group to try and work out what the following words mean and write their *definitions* on the paper:

ASSOT	(Stupid)
MAW-WALLOP	(Badly cooked)
WOWF	(Really stupid)
FRAMPOLD	(Boisterous)
SORNER	(To scrounge)
CURKLING	(To cry)
GELID	(Cold)
GOTCH-GUT	(Fat)
PUKKA	(Genuine)
FUGLE	(To cheat)
FRANGIBLE	(Delicate)
NINNYHAMMER	(Fool)
BRINDIZE	(To drink)
BARRELASS	(To fall)
LOOBY	(Clumsy)

And yes, all of the words are real but not used too often!

Once you've finished reading all of the words ask the group to give some of their definitions before you reveal what the word really means!

(Allow 10 minutes for this activity.)

Many things which we read or hear often need a bit of explanation. Why not take a look at 'You're softening my heart' (*The Australian Worship Collection*, 137) or 'I have heard of your fame' (*The Australian Worship Collection*, 30).

(Allow 5 minutes for this.)

Ask the group what they thought the lyrics of the chosen song meant.

Read Matthew 3:1-12.

Can you imagine what image John the Baptist would have made? Just think, here's a bloke dressed in a camel-hair suit, a leather strap wrapped around his waist and dipping grasshoppers into a pot of honey and popping them into his mouth! In between mouthfuls he gives the crowd a load of verbal about their antics and suggests they have a lot in common with snakes. He then goes on to give them some tips on gardening and hints that they all could do with a dunk in the river. You can just hear the mutterings of 'Been in the sun too long' or 'What can you expect from someone who wanders around the desert all day?' Quite a few folk would have been making gestures indicating that John was a few grains short of a sand-castle.

John the Baptist was a man who had turned his back on the comforts that most people enjoyed and had given himself to reading and meditating about God. Despite his odd appearance and behaviour, John was recognised as a messenger. His message was that all the people should '. . . Get the road ready for the Lord . . .' (Matthew 3:3). This wasn't such a strange thing to say as you might imagine. During, and before, biblical times the roads were almost non-existent. Those tracks that did exist were in a terrible condition and most people who travelled were warned to sort out all their legal affairs and say goodbye to their family because there was no guarantee that you would get to your intended destination safely.

The few good roads that did exist were built for a special purpose. King Solomon built a road of black basalt (a volcanic rock which often contained crystals). These special roads were constructed to reflect the wealth of the king. These roads were built by the king and mainly for the benefit of the king. They were often referred to as 'The king's highway'. Before the king began his travels a message was sent out telling the people to get the roads repaired and looking good in preparation for the king's arrival.

John's message was just the same, the only difference being that the road to be prepared wasn't made of basalt but of flesh and blood, the human heart and mind. John was preparing the people to hear the words of Jesus and the words wouldn't reach their destination if the 'road' wasn't ready to receive a message from the King.

John was concerned that the people were too occupied with their own comforts and had forgotten who God was! The rulers, politicians and religious leaders were too busy building their own little kingdoms to listen to the message of the 'King'. John was determined that when Jesus began his journey the people had at least been warned of his coming.

Ask the group to spend a few moments thinking about these questions:

- How do we respond to people who are different from us?
- Why do we respond in this way to people who are different?
- Should we all be the same?
- Are we all the same?

Place a large sheet of paper (A3) on the wall. Stick images of different people/cultures/communities/places on to the paper as a collage. It might have more impact if you ask a question and then place an image on to the paper, and continue with question/image until all the images are on the wall.

While the group are still in a quiet or reflective mood, read the following prayer:

Lord,
    I quite like the colour green.
It reminds me of spring and summer
    and of all those nice bits of the year
    that make me feel OK.
I'm not too keen on blue, purple
    or even pink.
These are the kind of colours that
    remind me of a dodgy trifle
    where all the colours have mixed together
    and formed a right old mess,
    something best eaten with the lights out.
Don't you think people are a bit like that?
All sorts of colours,
    races, ideas, creeds and beliefs
    all mixed together in a cosmopolitan stew.
That kind of mix may be all right for
    sociologists, anthropologists and psychologists,
    but isn't it a bit much for people like me
    to understand
    each and every one,
    every like, dislike,
    idea, taste, culture, tradition and point of view?
I mean, come on,
    play fair.
You can't expect me
    to understand
    what makes everybody tick.
I really haven't got the time for that,
    or even the motivation
    to stretch my brain
    beyond breaking point.
So, if it's OK with you

can I be the one
who's in the right,
does the right thing,
at the right time,
for all the right reasons?
And can I be the only one
who's got the answer,
to what's wrong with the rest of the world?
And can I be the one
who is on the side of justice,
hope and freedom,
standing against hypocrisy,
discrimination and injustice?
'Cos you know that I'm
the way everyone should be,
don't you?
But then again,
I suppose all sorts of people,
all over the place,
could be asking the same thing,
from the same point of view,
thinking that they're
the way everyone else should be.
Lord,
I think we're all a bit mixed up,
and perhaps it's better this way,
that we're all different, but the same.
Having the same needs,
hurts, pains, hang-ups,
and longing
to be loved
for who we are,
without judgement,
without prejudice,
without hypocrisy.
I suppose
when I think about it,
I like lots of colours really.
It would be extremely boring
for everything to be the same,
without any shades or texture
to differentiate
between one and the other.
Lord,
thanks that we're not the same
and give me the kind of understanding
that springs from a heart
that wants to be
what you want me to be.

The good news of Jesus _____

Mark 1:1-8: John prepares the way for Jesus

Equipment:
cards, or sheets of paper with parts of headlines written in large letters
paper and pens
candle

Distribute the cards to each member of the group. (Some members may have more than one card.) Divide the group into twos or threes. Ask each group to try and make 'headlines' using the words on their cards. Can anyone make up a story to match the headline?

Headline words:

One man	Purple shoes	for	the
Toffee ice-cream	Mild explosion	and	an
Escaped budgie	in	today	
Last night	Runs around	with	
Toothless monkey	yesterday	next	
Hours	Rubber bucket	of	
Attempts to fly	in	a	

(Allow 10 minutes for this activity.)

Ask the group to think quickly of one or two current TV adverts. Can they remember the catch line or 'hook' for the adverts? It is important to market a product or service as effectively as possible. Unfortunately some companies didn't get it quite right:

- Scandinavian vacuum manufacturer Electrolux used the following advert in America: 'Nothing sucks like an Electrolux!'
- In Taiwan, the translation of the Pepsi slogan 'Come alive with Pepsi' came out as 'Pepsi will bring your ancestors back from the dead!'
- In China, the Kentucky Fried Chicken slogan: 'finger-lickin' good' was translated as 'eat your fingers off!'
- In Italy, a campaign for Schweppes Tonic Water translated the name into 'Schweppes Toilet Water!'

Getting the right message across is important.

(Allow 5 minutes for this activity.)

Read Mark 1:1-8.

The Gospel of Mark is written in a journalistic style giving us short 'news' stories relating to Jesus. John the Baptist began to declare the coming of the 'Good News' against a background of political and civil unrest. The Romans had been in control of Judea since approximately 63 BC. Roman rule was often directed through local kings as a way of trying to put an acceptable 'face' on the Roman occupation. The most famous of these local rulers was Herod the Great, who was king when Jesus was born.

Under Roman rule trade prospered within a single market that stretched from France to Egypt and North Africa. Within this trade area there was relative peace, enforced by harsh penalties for those who 'broke' Roman law. For most Jews there was another negative aspect of the Roman occupation, that of taxation. It is thought that the Jewish public paid out almost half of their income in taxes. Every Jewish male had to pay a tax for the maintenance of the Temple and to keep the priests in food and clothes. To make matters worse, the Romans imposed taxes which included a poll tax, a land tax and a sales tax. It wasn't surprising that several groups who opposed Roman domination were waiting for an opportunity to get rid of the Romans.

In the reading from Mark, we are introduced to John the Baptist who, quoting from the Old Testament, declared 'Clear a path in the desert! Make a straight road for the Lord our God' (Isaiah 40:3). John the Baptist was the 'advertising campaign' for Jesus. He was calling people back to God and everywhere John went crowds gathered to hear what he had to say. The heart of John's message was about Jesus. His, John's, role was to prepare the way and get the attention of the people, to prepare them heart and mind for the 'Good News'.

(Allow 10 minutes.)

Some advertising campaigns use catchy slogans while others use visual images to 'get the message across'. John the Baptist was an extremely effective 'advert' for Jesus: in his actions and in what he said. Ask the group to separate into twos or threes and write a one-sentence headline which John the Baptist might have used to announce the coming of the 'Good News'.

(Allow 5 minutes for this activity.)

Place a candle in the centre of the room. As you light the candle read:

> Once again Jesus spoke to the people. This time he said, 'I am the light of the world! Follow me, and you won't be walking in the dark. You will have the light that gives you life.' (John 8:12)

Ask the group to look at the candle and consider what the words of Jesus mean to them. What kind of 'advert' in words or actions are they for Jesus?

How can they be an 'advert' for Jesus? As the group consider these questions and look at the candle, read:

Then Jesus said to all the people: 'If any of you want to be my followers, you must forget about yourself. You must take up your cross each day and follow me. If you want to save your life, you will destroy it. But if you give up your life for me, you will save it. What will you gain, if you own the whole world but destroy yourself or waste your life?' (Luke 9:23-27)

Turning on the heat _____

Luke 3:7-18: The message of John the Baptist

Equipment:
plastic carrier bag
music and lyrics

Welcome the group as normal but – your appearance is far from normal!

Make sure that you are only dressed in a pair of shorts and a ripped T-shirt. Once the group have sat down and given you some odd looks, apologise for the way you are dressed (or not!). Explain that you have had a bad time and all you have left in the world is what they see. Don't offer any explanation for your 'loss'.

Pick up the plastic carrier bag and hold it out in front of you. With a sad expression on your face, politely ask the group if any of them would be willing to give you some essential items such as socks, shoes, jumper, coat. Place any(!) donated items in the bag.

(Allow ten minutes for this activity.)

Does someone's 'odd' behaviour make you feel uncomfortable? How do we react to expressions of eccentric behaviour?

See what you think of 'These are the days' by Robin Mark (*Re:source 2000*, 14) or 'The Spirit of the Lord' by Graham Kendrick (*Re:source 2000*, 15).

(Allow approximately five minutes.)

Ask the group what they thought of your behaviour. Did it embarrass them? Or did they think it was a funny stunt? Would they have responded differently if it had been real?

Read Luke 3:7-18.
You have to imagine the scene: out of the desert comes this large, hairy man, dressed in clothes made of camel's hair, a leather strap around his waist and living on a diet of grasshoppers and wild honey (see Matthew 3:4). Not only does he look a tiny bit different, but he's shouting his head off about all manner of things!

After quoting the prophet Isaiah, John then goes on to call a load of people 'snakes who come running from judgement'.

John had spent a long time in the desert, some might say too long! The desert was covered in brushwood, twigs and dry stalks of dead plants. At times a spark could set the desert alight, burning anything that could be burnt. When this happened, it was common for vipers to slither out of the nooks and crannies where they lay hidden, and attempt to escape the flames. It was this picture that John must have had in his head when the people rushed to hear what he had to say. Some thought he was the Messiah, a claim he quickly denied by saying that he was not good enough to untie the sandals of the one to come. (The act of undoing someone's sandals was the act of a servant.)

The people who came to John wanted to know what they had to do to escape the 'coming judgement' (see verse 7). John didn't tell them to get down and pray, go to church as often as they could or read the scripture continuously; he directed his comments at their lifestyle. John told the tax collectors not to overcharge to line their own pockets, he told the soldiers not to charge protection money and he told those who were well-off to share what they had with the poor. These were all issues that Jesus later tackled.

John was trying to make it clear that just appearing to act 'godly', by going to church, reading the Bible and praying, was not what God required. God wanted a change of heart which would be reflected by the way people lived.

What do the group think about the way that John spoke to the people who came to see him? Wasn't he making enemies rather than encouraging people to turn back to God and be baptised (verse 3)? Eventually, John did use a few too many words when he criticised Herod Antipas, ruler of the area, for marrying Herodias (who was, at one time, Herod's sister-in-law and his niece). Herod Antipas met Herodias, who was married to another bloke called . . . Herod. He seduced her and later married her. Now, Herod Antipas was related to Herod who was married to Herodias (!) In one way and another, Herod, Herod Antipas and Herodias were all related through Herod the Great. It gets confusing (not to mention a severe lack of imagination when it comes to names), but by the standards of Jewish law and opinion the marriage of Herod Antipas and Herodias was well out of order. Using a few choice words, John the Baptist pointed out that Herod Antipas' actions were wrong, which resulted in John being shoved in prison for his failure to compromise his message.

Are there any areas of our lives where John's lack of compromise would embarrass us?

Ask the group to consider areas of their lives about which John might have a few choice words to say. While the group think about these issues, ask them to imagine God asking them to turn their backs on these areas and walk away, with the confidence of having God's arm around their shoulders.

After a period of quiet, read Psalm 25:1-10:

I offer you my heart, Lord God, and I trust you.
Don't make me ashamed or let enemies defeat me.
Don't disappoint any of your worshippers,
    but disappoint all deceitful liars.
Show me your paths and teach me to follow;
    guide me by your truth and instruct me.
You keep me safe, and I always trust you.

Please, Lord, remember,
    you have always been patient and kind.
Forget each wrong I did when I was young.
Show how truly kind you are and remember me.
You are honest and merciful,
    and you teach sinners how to follow your path.
You lead humble people to do what is right
    and to stay on your path.
In everything you do, you are kind and faithful
    to everyone who keeps our agreement with you.

Ordinarily extraordinary

Luke 1:39-45: Mary visits Elizabeth

Equipment:
postcards
music and lyrics
large sheet of paper

Write one of the statements below on each postcard.

1. A giraffe can clean its ears with its 52-centimetre tongue.
2. Fingernails grow nearly four times faster than toenails.
3. Clinophobia is the fear of beds.
4. A mole can dig a 100-metre tunnel in just one night.
5. Slugs have four noses.
6. A sneeze travels out of your nose at over 100 miles per hour.
7. The elephant is the only mammal that can't jump.
8. More *Monopoly* money is printed in a year than real money.
9. More people use blue toothbrushes than red ones.
10. No piece of paper can be folded in half more than seven times.

Give the cards to group members and ask them to read the statement on the card. They can then ask the rest of the group whether they think the statement is true or false. (All the statements are true . . . check them out!)

(Allow 10 minutes for this activity.)

Some statements just seem far too weird to be true. Some facts can be proven, some can be disproved and others we may never understand.

Take a look at 'You have taken the precious' by Kevin Prosch and Tom Davis (*The Source*, 600) or 'From heaven you came' by Graham Kendrick (*The Source*, 114).

(Allow approximately 5 minutes.)

What did the group think about the lyrics of the chosen song? Are there statements that take a bit of thinking about or seem too difficult to take in?

Read Luke 1:39-45.

Most people are really pleased when someone tells them about an eagerly awaited pregnancy. There's weeks of planning and preparation, every conversation seems to be centred around the coming event and it's hard to think about anything else (especially if you're the parents!).

It's much the same for an unplanned pregnancy, except that the conversation isn't always too encouraging! In fact, the conversation, or gossip, isn't always very complimentary.

You can imagine how Mary felt. Here she was, a teenager, engaged to a respectable bloke and along pops an angel to tell her she's pregnant. It didn't help matters that she came from an area that had a bit of a rough reputation to start with. Mary came from Nazareth, which was considered to be a no-go area for any respectable Jew. Nazareth was full of non-Jews (and some Jews) who didn't observe all the requirements of the Jewish law. Nazareth also attracted 'foreigners' who brought with them customs and traditions that were thought to be a bit dodgy for Jews.

So, after discovering that she is pregnant, Mary goes off to another town to visit her cousin Elizabeth. Elizabeth's husband is a priest and is respected in his community. Elizabeth opens the door and immediately Mary greets her with the news that she's engaged to Joseph (how nice for you, dear!), she's a virgin (Joseph will be pleased) and she's pregnant (Joseph will definitely not be pleased).

You would imagine Elizabeth would be shocked but she isn't! Instead her baby (born to be John the Baptist) moves in her womb and Elizabeth celebrates the news!

Elizabeth isn't a stranger to the unusual. She and her husband, Zechariah, were both harvesting wrinkles (getting old) and didn't have any children, and this in a society that considered children a blessing and to be without children a punishment from God.

Put simply, Zechariah moaned to God about not having children, God sent an angel to tell Zechariah that Elizabeth would have a son, Elizabeth became pregnant, Zechariah moaned to God (who said 'typical man'?), and God caused Zechariah to be dumb (lucky Elizabeth) until the birth of John.

Because of her own situation, Elizabeth was able to understand what Mary was going through and called her 'fortunate' because Mary chose to believe God. Both Elizabeth and Mary chose to believe and trust in God in situations that were far from normal.

Ask the group to imagine how Zechariah might have reacted to Mary's news. He is a respected member of the community and his wife's cousin arrives with some disturbing news. Could he have thought: 'Well, what do you expect, coming from Nazareth?' or 'What are the other priests going to say about this?'

How do we react to news that's a little hard to believe or is something we don't really want to hear? Do we dismiss it straightaway or think for a few seconds and then dismiss it?

(Allow 5 minutes.)

Place a large sheet of paper on the wall. Draw a large question mark on the paper. Ask the group to look at the question mark. Ask them whether they treat information or situations that they don't understand as untrue or wrong purely because they cannot relate to what they're hearing.

Ask everyone to spend a few moments in reflection while you read the following Bible verses:

Psalm 86:11-13.
Teach me to follow you, and I will obey your truth.
Always keep me faithful.
With all my heart I thank you.
I praise you, Lord God.
Your love for me is so great
    that you protect me from death and the grave.

A startling piece of news! _____

Luke 1:26-38: An angel tells about the birth of Jesus

Equipment:
a piece of card for each member of the group
a pen for every group member

On each card write a job title. Use a variety of job titles, combining the sensible with the totally wacky! For example, doctor, teacher, politician, dustman, window cleaner, waiter, toilet attendant, couch potato, tea taster, deck chair attendant, pig farmer.

Give a card to each member of the group. Ask them to look at the card and, if they are happy with the job title, keep the card. If they would rather exchange it for another card, they can try and persuade someone else to exchange cards but neither person should know what is on the other's card!

When all the 'bartering' has finished ask the group how they felt about receiving the original card and, if they exchanged it, were they any happier with the new card?

(Allow 10 minutes for this activity.)

Read the following news stories. After each one ask the group if they think it is true or false. Don't tell them if they are right or wrong. When you have read the last story tell them that every story was in fact true!

1. A policeman responded to a report of a robbery at a local school. When he arrived three teenagers started to run away. The policeman, knowing he couldn't catch them, shouted, 'Stop or I'll set my dog on to you' (even though he didn't have a dog). The teenagers kept on running. So, the policeman took the idea one stage further and began barking. Immediately the three teenagers stopped running and gave themselves up!

2. A man in New Mexico got drunk and started to shoot at giant cacti. One fell on him!

3. A man walked into a newsagent's shop and put a twenty pound note on the counter and asked for it to be changed. When the newsagent opened the cash register the man pulled out a gun and demanded the contents of the cash register. He took the cash and ran out of the shop, leaving the twenty pound note on the counter. He escaped with fifteen pounds!

(Allow approximately 5 minutes.)

The group may have guessed that the stories were all true. They may even know of stranger stories! We are used to hearing all sorts of weird and wonderful stories. It's quite possible that Mary had heard a few wacky stories as well. But nothing could have prepared her for the visit of the Angel Gabriel.

Read Luke 1:26-38.

The Angel Gabriel greets Mary and says, 'You are truly blessed! The Lord is with you.' There are two things to note here. First, meeting with an angel was not an everyday occurrence! So this would have put Mary in a bit of a spin. Second, the Angel Gabriel told Mary that the Lord had blessed her! She somehow had found favour with God! She was confused and must have wondered what on earth was going on. The angel notes that Mary is a bit confused and tells her not to worry: 'Don't be afraid'. This is not a gentle pat on the hand or 'Shall we have a cup of tea and talk this over?' No! The Angel Gabriel launches straight in with, 'The Lord is pleased with you and you're going to have a baby. He will be called the Son of God the Most High!' Well, of course this happens to every young woman! Doesn't it? At this point Mary is really feeling the heat. First, she is greeted by an angel. Second, she is told that she is blessed by God and then told she's going to have a baby who will rule the people of Israel! And this is before she is even married!

Mary was engaged to Joseph. The normal engagement lasted about a year and was as legally binding as being married. The engagement could only be broken off through a divorce. Mary listened to the Angel Gabriel's message and answered, 'I am the Lord's servant! Let it happen as you have said'. Mary didn't want to argue with God. She recognised that God had chosen her to do something special for him. She didn't know the full story or have a complete picture of what was going to happen. She didn't know how Joseph would react to the news. She didn't even know why God had chosen her for this task. Mary placed her trust in God.

Ask the group to think of something they would like to achieve in the future or a job they would like to do, and to write it down on the back of the 'job cards'. Can each member of the group trust God to sort out the future for them?

(Allow 5 minutes for this task.)

Suggest the group might like to consider their future and God's role in that during the reading of Psalm 25:1-5.

I offer you my heart, Lord God, and I trust you.
Don't make me ashamed or let enemies defeat me.
Don't disappoint any of your worshippers, but disappoint all deceitful liars.
Show me your paths and teach me to follow;
     guide me by your truth and instruct me.
You keep me safe, and I always trust you.
Amen.

A different kind of lamb!

Luke 2:15-21: The shepherds hear about Jesus

Equipment:
large cards or A4 sheets
music and lyrics or drama sketch

Take ten cards and write the following headlines:

'Budgie eats tube of Smarties!'

'Sales of coloured tissues drop'

'Two injured in ice-cream fight!'

'Forty witnesses to chocolate bar theft'

'Lorry carrying paint overturns. Multicoloured motorway'

'Police fear local car thief may strike again'

'Government declare national holiday every Monday'

'Island disappears after volcanic eruption'

'United Nations calls for world-wide nuclear testing ban'

'Local man swallows Guinness book of records!'

Show each headline to the group. For each headline ask the group whether it should be reported in the local newspaper or national newspaper; on local radio or national radio; local TV or national TV?

(Allow 10 minutes.)

Have a listen to 'Our God is great' by Dave Bilbrough (*The Source 2*, 933). Alternatively, look at 'Mighty God' by Mark Johnson, Helen Johnson and Chris Bowater (*The Source*, 356). You might like to use another piece of music which reflects the theme of 'news'. Have a copy of the lyrics available.

(Allow approximately 5 minutes.)

News seems to travel fast, particularly when it may be something that we would like kept quiet!

Discuss the lyrics or drama sketch. Why are we interested in knowing what goes on everywhere? Who is the first person we tell our 'news' to? You can chat about some of the news stories which are sold to the highest bidder according to their news 'value', i.e. will it increase sales or audience figures?

Read Luke 2:15-21.

Would you have chosen shepherds to tell this news to? Shepherds didn't enjoy a good press in Biblical times. The shepherds were thought to be amongst the lowest form of worker around. The nature of the job meant that the shepherds spent more time with sheep than they did with people! Their job was demanding and didn't allow them to observe all the rituals and traditions of religious worship. It's interesting that the news about the birth of Jesus should be told to people who were not seen as the best representatives of the Jewish faith!

It is quite likely that these shepherds were 'Temple' shepherds. These were shepherds who looked after the Temple's private sheep flocks. The flocks mentioned in the reading were kept in pastures close to Bethlehem. The shepherds' duty was to look after the lambs and present a flawless lamb for morning and evening sacrifice.

The angels came to tell the news to the shepherds who were amongst the first to hear of the birth; not the kind of people who would automatically be the first to be told other 'important' news. Another interesting point to make is that these shepherds, who were responsible for providing the sacrificial lambs, were introduced to the Lamb of God, the ultimate sacrifice (see John 1:29).

The angels didn't just come to tell the shepherds about the birth. It was custom that when a baby boy was born the local musicians would go to the house and welcome the new-born boy by singing simple songs. As Jesus was born in a stable, away from his parents' home, this custom could not have ordinarily been carried out. It seems that God arranged for some extra-ordinary singers and musicians to welcome the birth of Jesus!

Ask the group to consider a possible 'headline' which gives a good insight into the Bible reading. Try to brainstorm some ideas quickly and agree upon a headline which everyone feels sums up the reading.

(Allow 5 minutes for this task.)

Suggest to the group that they might like to close their eyes and picture the scene where the angels are singing praise to God while the shepherds watch in amazement. While the group are quiet, read Psalm 136.

Praise the Lord! He is good.
God's love never fails.
Praise the God of all gods.
God's love never fails.
Praise the Lord of lords.
God's love never fails.
Only God works great miracles.
God's love never fails.

What a dream!

Matthew 1:18-25: The birth of Jesus

Equipment:
paper
pens

Distribute a pen and paper to everyone in the group. Ask them to think about an odd or strange dream that they've had recently (you may have to verbally edit some dreams!). Tell them to write one sentence at the top of the paper and then fold the top of the paper over so that the writing cannot be seen. They should then pass the paper to the person on their left and then, once everyone has exchanged papers, they write a second sentence about their dream. Continue to fold the paper over after each added sentence and exchange papers until the written accounts of their dreams have finished (this may take a bit of co-ordination as not all dreams will be of the same length). Ask the group to exchange papers one more time and then each member of the group should read the dream story that appears on the piece of paper. The result should be a little bit weird!

(Allow 10 minutes for this activity.)

It may be a cliché, but different things do mean different things to different people. God can speak to us using words, ideas or situations so that he can communicate with us in a way we can understand and appreciate.

Have a look at 'We will seek you first' (*The American Worship Collection*, 98) or 'We lift our voices' (*The American Worship Collection*, 94).
(Allow 5 minutes.)

We all have dreams of one sort or another. Sometimes those dreams are extremely vivid and we remember them throughout the day. Other times, we can hardly remember anything about the dream but we are left with a curious feeling, not quite being able to explain why we feel this way but, somehow our subconscious decided to delve into the far reaches of our mind and project thoughts and images onto our cinematic sleep-time.

Read Matthew 1:18-25.
Joseph had a dream . . . a great, stonking, technicolour, 3-D, front row sort.

slapper

Imagine, here's a bloke who's just found out that the woman he was engaged to is pregnant! You know how it is, take it in your stride, no problem, happens every day. Wrong!

The Jewish tradition was for the marriage to be taken in three stages. Firstly, an engagement was often announced while the couple were still children, their engagement having been arranged by the children's parents. Second was the 'betrothal'. This was the official bit which lasted a year and could only be called off if the female was unwilling to go ahead before the formal agreement had been announced. To break off the 'betrothal' was only possible by divorce. The third part was the actual marriage ceremony, which occurred at the end of the year of betrothal.

Tradition had ruled that if a woman was pregnant before marriage then she was considered to be promiscuous and could, after a public trial, be stoned to death. Fortunately, at the time of Mary and Joseph's betrothal, stoning had become history (to a large cheer of relief from a percentage of the female population). It was now custom to conduct a 'secret' divorce and keep the problem as far from wagging tongues as possible. This was the action that Joseph had decided upon before the dream.

So, there he goes, off to bed with a cluttered head full of angry thoughts and feelings of rejection. Then, just as soon as his eyelids hit the cheeks, along comes a gold-framed dream direct from God. Can you imagine, God tells him that it's still OK to marry Mary, she may be pregnant but she hadn't been unfaithful to him and she was still a virgin! Having received all of this, Joseph turned over and carried on snoozing . . . no he didn't! Joseph listened to what he'd heard and did exactly as God had asked him to. He married Mary even though a lot of people would have suggested that he hadn't been able to wait until his marriage before starting a family or that he'd failed to follow customs of the Jewish law and walked in the opposite direction to Mary.

Joseph heard God, did as he was asked and kept faith in God's word. God had used a dream to get through to Joseph and the dream had packed a real punch. Joseph was to remember that dream many times during Mary's pregnancy and afterwards.

Is it possible that we too can hear from God, do exactly as he asks and stick with it even when the gossip suggests that we may be a few biscuits short of a packet? A few years ago, before crossing the road, children were encouraged to 'Stop! Look! And Listen!' Not a bad piece of advice especially when God wants to have a word in our ear.

Dreams often feature ours fears, hurts, hopes or a mixture of all three! Ask the group if any of them would be willing to share with everyone an ambition or hope which they have. It may be that someone is hoping to pass their exams and continue their studies but are afraid of failing; it might be that someone feels hurt at being left out of an event that they were looking forward to being a part of. Whatever it may be, you can use this time to encourage that person and maybe offer to help, pray for or just be someone who'll listen to the hassles.

Also, use part of this time to answer one of the questions that one of the group raised last time.

Ask the group to be quiet for a few moments while you read the following prayer:

Lord,
　　it's quite a crazy thought
　　that somewhere
　　in the technicolour maze
　　of my dreams, that somehow, somewhere,
　　you might want to have a word with me!
I think I'm a bit embarrassed really.
My dreams are what you might call
　　a visual dustbin,
　　a montage of funny bits, dodgy bits,
　　gruesome bits and just plain wacky bits.
I have other dreams of course.
The sort where I want to do
　　all kinds of exciting things,
　　go to exciting places,
　　meet loads of different people
　　and immediately forget their names.
There's so much I want to do
　　but I'd sort of
　　want your opinion on things.
So if you don't mind,
　　can we talk about it,
　　think about it
　　and even dream about it?
'Cos I'm not so sure
　　that I can get through this on my own.
Be with me, Lord,
　　guide my ways
　　and help me through
　　whatever comes my way.

Wise up!

Matthew 2:1-12: The wise men

Equipment:
sticky labels
pen and paper for each person
music and lyrics

Before the group arrive write the following words onto the sticky labels:

Friday	Christmas	Father	Baby
Deer	Old	Uncle	Auntie
Computer	Mug	Tree	Paper
Sweet	Sour	Pie	Custard

You can add more items to suit the number of the group. As the group arrive stick one of the labels on their backs, but don't tell them what it is. Tell everyone to move around and ask other members of the group, 'What is my label?' The other group members have to mime the item and can only answer yes or no to questions. When someone has guessed correctly what their label is they can sit down and watch the others trying to guess theirs.

(Allow 10 minutes for this activity.)

It can be extremely frustrating knowing that the answer to your dilemma is literally behind you but you have to depend on other people to tell you what it is.

Have a look at 'We will glorify' (*The American Worship Collection*, 97) or 'With our hearts' (*The American Worship Collection*, 103).

(Allow 5 minutes for this.)

Take a look at the lyrics to the song and ask the group if the words meant anything to them.

Read Matthew 2:1-12.
When people buy presents for us they usually have a good idea of our likes and dislikes, favourite music, clothes and current rave chocolate bar. The choice of present isn't just a random 'pick anything off the shelf and hope

it's OK' type of thing. Presents are given with the hope that the recipient will appreciate (and possibly really like) the choice of gift which will earn the buyer a heartfelt 'thank you'. More often than not, we can even guess what certain people will buy or give us as a present. You know, Gran always buys you a book token equivalent to the price of a book in 1920 while Uncle Arthur never fails to give you a crumpled paper bag containing a selection of boiled sweets. And, on a good year, Great Aunt Dot will give you a box of patterned handkerchiefs which she received for Christmas two years ago.

Often the selection of a present has been given lots of thought and chosen to 'fit' the recipient. Usually a present means something, even if it is only a 'Look, I remembered!'

The wise men didn't just happen to be passing the stable where the infant Jesus was. Neither did they hear about his birth and rush down to the nearest shop and pull any old thing off the shelf. Each present was given for a reason, to mean something, to reflect something of the character of the recipient.

Gold has always represented royalty and still does. In Old Testament times it was also a sign of holiness.

Frankincense was a very desirable perfume. It was used by the Jewish priests in the Temple who acted as the 'middle-men' between God and the people.

Myrrh was another perfume used to relieve pain and to anoint the dead prior to burial.

Each of the wise men's gifts represented something of the character of Jesus. He was a Holy King who would act as the bridge-builder between God and the people and would eventually suffer and die as a sacrifice.

The wise men had travelled a great distance to bring their gifts. They knew something of the character of the infant and each gift had a particular significance.

For each of us, Jesus himself became a gift. He became the once and for all sacrifice that would enable us to form an eternal relationship with God. Now, that's a gift that really means something!

Give each member of the group a piece of paper and a pen. Chat about what everyone thinks would be the ideal, totally most awesome present. After that, ask everyone to imagine that they are a present which is going to be given to someone they respect, love or admire. What kind of present would they be? Ask them to write their idea onto their piece of paper. Secondly, get everyone to think about what gift they would be if they wanted to make a difference in somebody's life. For example, if they wanted to make a difference to the life of someone who was physically unable to leave their home, they might like to be a car so that they could transport the housebound person wherever they wanted to go. Write the second idea down onto the piece of paper. Compare the two ideas. How different are they? When we are buying a present does it make a difference whether we know the people very well or not?

Suggest to the group that it would be a good idea to be quiet for a few moments and to think what they could do to help people who are in need of some care and attention. While the group are quiet read the following Psalm:

Psalm 107:1-9, 43
Shout praises to the Lord!
He is good to us, and his love never fails.
Everyone the Lord has rescued from trouble should praise him,
    everyone he has brought from the east and the west,
    the north and the south.
Some of you were lost in the scorching desert, far from a town.
You were hungry and thirsty and about to give up.
You were in serious trouble,
    but you prayed to the Lord, and he rescued you.
Straightaway he brought you to a town.
You should praise the Lord for his love
    and for the wonderful things he does for all of us.
To everyone who is thirsty, he gives something to drink;
    to everyone who is hungry, he gives good things to eat . . .
Be wise! Remember this and think about the kindness of the Lord.

All in a dream

Matthew 2:13-23: The escape to Egypt

Equipment:
postcards
paper
pens
envelope
music and lyrics

Write statement one (below) on the first postcard, statement two on the second postcard and so on until all the statements have been written on postcards (you might like to add some of your own statements too).

1. Over 2500 left-handed people are killed each year in the USA, from using products made for right-handed people.
2. If you were to count for 24 hours a day, it would take 31,688 years to reach one trillion.
3. A crocodile always grows new teeth to replace the old teeth.
4. The sentence: 'The quick brown fox jumps over the lazy dog,' uses every letter of the alphabet.
5. The only fifteen-letter word that can be spelt without repeating a letter is 'Uncopyrightable'.
6. A hedgehog's heart beats 300 times a minute on average.
7. Camels have three eyelids to protect themselves from sand blowing into their eyes.
8. Ancient Egyptians slept on pillows made of stone.
9. Around 1000 BC, most Egyptians were dead before their thirtieth birthday.
10. Every time you lick a stamp you are consuming one tenth of a calorie.

Give each member of the group a piece of paper and a pen. Distribute the cards, one to each member of the group, and ask them to read the statement on the card. They then ask the rest of the group whether they think the statement is true or false. After each statement each group member writes their answer on the piece of paper. Once all the statements have been read you can reveal that they are all true. Total the scores and see who has the most correct answers.

(Allow 10 minutes for this activity.)

Behaving in the way that we feel God is asking us to requires a lot of courage. If anybody tells you it's easy you have permission to ignore them!

Try looking at 'I trust in you, my faithful Lord' (*The Source 2*, 804) or 'Come, now is the time to worship' (*The Source 2*, 662).

(Allow 5 minutes for this.)

Ask the group what they thought of the lyrics to the chosen song. What point were the lyrics trying to make?

Read Matthew 2:13-23.

No sooner had Joseph started to get his head around the idea of a pregnant girlfriend than three wise men turn up with gifts that weren't cuddly, couldn't feed the baby, and certainly wouldn't treat nappy rash!

At some stage Joseph must have dreamt of a normal, traditional betrothal, a nice wedding where aunties cried while uncles drank the wine, and the beginning of a marriage where lots of people gave them gifts and threw confetti . . . or rice, or dates, or orange pips or something. But God had other ideas for Joseph and his bride.

God had already spoken to Joseph in a dream to assure him that Mary was faithful and that the child she would eventually give birth to was special. Now, after using a dream to warn the wise men to make a detour on the way home, God speaks to Joseph again through a dream. So, Joseph and his new family take a long holiday in Egypt, where Joseph has another dream (quite a while later) telling him to go home to Israel then another dream telling them to go and live in Nazareth!

The Bible doesn't tell us whether Joseph had a habit of eating vast quantities of cheese before he went to bed but he certainly had some vivid dreams! But, the most important point is that Joseph was obedient to what he felt God was telling him to do. Even though Joseph would almost certainly have felt fazed, anxious, frightened and a few fries short of a happy meal, he still placed his trust in God. Each time he listened and obeyed God Joseph was building his confidence in what God said and did. Often Joseph wouldn't have a clue what God was up to; he still went ahead and built his faith in God each step of the way. There would have been a lot of criticism and pointing fingers but Joseph was learning to trust in a God who kept his promises.

Ask the group what things or actions they feel unable to trust God with. Suggest that the group write their answers on a piece of paper, fold them up and place them in an envelope.

Put the envelope in the centre of the room and ask the group to be quiet for a few moments while you read the following Psalm:

Psalm 37:4-8, 23-24
Do what the Lord wants,
    and he will give you your heart's desire.
Let the Lord lead you and trust him to help.
Then it will be as clear as the noonday sun that you were right.
Be patient and trust the Lord.
Don't let it bother you when all goes well for those who do sinful things.
Don't be angry or furious. Anger leads to sin . . .
If you do what the Lord wants,
    he will make certain each step you take is sure.
The Lord will hold your hand,
    and if you stumble, you still won't fall.

Including you!

Luke 2:41-52: The boy Jesus in the temple

Equipment:
postcards
paper and pens
envelopes
music and lyrics

On the postcards write the following categories:

Short	Tall
Rabbit	Chicken
Stream	Pond
Athlete	Singer
Coffee	Tea
Porsche	Land-Rover

Divide the group in two and ask them to choose which of the categories they would like to be. For instance, if the categories chosen are 'Rabbit' and 'Chicken' then one half of the group will be rabbits and the other half chickens. You may need to 'help' the groups decide who is to be either the rabbit or the chicken. Give each group a sheet of paper and a pen and ask them to write down a list of qualities for their word. What are the benefits of being a rabbit? What's good about being a chicken?

Ask one member of each group to read their group's list of qualities and the other group can offer reasons why it is better to be in the other category.

Repeat the process with the other categories.

(Allow 10 minutes for this activity.)

What criteria do we use to make the kind of judgements that were made in the previous activity?

Have a look at 'When the music fades' by Matt Redman (*Re:source 2000*, 16) or 'Lord, you have my heart' by Martin Smith (*The Source*, 341).

(Allow approximately 5 minutes.)

What did the group think the lyrics of the song were attempting to say?

Read Luke 2:41-52.
Before we start to think about this account, by Luke, of Jesus getting himself into grief with his parents, it's worth trying to understand a little of the background.

At the age of 12, a Jewish boy officially becomes a man and takes on the associated duties and obligations. Jesus and his parents had travelled to Jerusalem to attend his first Passover (a meal to commemorate the exodus of the Israelites from captivity in Egypt). When it was time to go home, the women would have travelled together and set out earlier than the men. The men would follow later and both parties would meet up at the evening camp. You can imagine that both Mary and Joseph thought Jesus was travelling with the other parent: 'I thought he was with you!' 'No, I thought he was with you!'

Eventually, Jesus was found in the temple where the Sanhedrin (the supreme Jewish court) was meeting in public to discuss religious and theological questions. After three days' search, Mary and Joseph found Jesus listening to the discussions and asking questions. It was significant that at the same time as he reached adulthood, Jesus also acknowledged who he was and who his father was (see verse 49).

Jesus became aware of his status as an adult and the value that God placed upon him. It was this knowledge that gave him the motivation to return home with his parents, continue to learn the trade of a carpenter and allow his future to remain secure in God's hands.

Give each member of the group a pen, some paper and an envelope. Ask them how they would have felt if they'd been made aware that they had a special purpose, something that would make a real difference in the world? Would they have been eager to get 'on with it' or would they keep their head down and hope it all went away?

Do any of the group feel that they have a talent or gift for something that excites them or encourages them to dream about their future? Suggest to the group that they should write their 'dream' down on the piece of paper. Below, ask them to write down some ideas about how they can achieve that 'dream'. When complete, fold the paper and place it in the envelope and seal it closed. Offer to keep the envelopes in a secure place (promise not to peep) and they can open the envelope in twelve months' time and see if they think the same and whether they've made any progress towards their 'dream'.

Encourage each member of the group to understand that each one of them is special and God wants the best for them.
(Allow 5 minutes.)

Once the group have given you the sealed envelopes, place them in a central place and ask the group to be quiet while you read the following prayer:

Lord, I know,
   no matter how I feel right now,
   whether it's a dustbin or a toilet,
   you see us for who we really are –
   precious people who you care for, every day.
It's difficult, I mean really difficult,
   to see above the mess and clutter
   that surrounds us.
I'm glad that you can see through the rubbish
   and look at my life with love.
Help me
   to trust,
   to see,
   to feel
   your love,
   no matter what I feel like.

This planet earth

John 1:1-9, 10-18: The Word of life

Equipment:
card
paper
pens
candles
match
music and lyrics

Listed below are all the major planets of our own sun. Firstly, the planets' names have been rearranged and, secondly, they are not in order according to distance. Each group member needs to unravel the planet's name and then list them in order of distance beginning with the nearest to the sun and furthest away from the sun.

1. Heart
2. Rams
3. Curry me
4. Nuves
5. Nutars
6. Lutop
7. Teen pun
8. Tierupj
9. Suruna

The correct order should be Mercury, Venus, Earth, Mars, Jupiter, Saturn, Uranus, Neptune, Pluto.

Distribute the paper and pens to the group and ask them to solve the planetary problem!

(Allow 10 minutes for this.)

It might not have been difficult to work out the jumbled letters of the planets but placing them in order of distance was, most probably, all guesswork!

Take a look at 'You laid aside your majesty' (*The Source*, 601) or 'All heaven declares' (*The Source*, 8).

(Allow 5 minutes for this.)

Take a look at the lyrics to your chosen song. What do they say about God?

Read John 1:1-9,10-18.

The whole solar system is so vast that even if we could map every single part of it the sheer complexity and variety would be virtually impossible to comprehend. It is all so awesome that rather than try and understand every minute detail it's easier just to simply stare at its beauty.

If you look at the night sky, the planets and stars, your senses are overwhelmed. Words fail to describe fully the vision before you. That's something like John the Baptist would have felt when he saw Jesus. Here was God's promise to humankind, in the flesh and offering one blessing after another (see verse 16). Just as the sun provides light and life for the earth, it shines on every one of us and even lights up the other planets without losing any of its brightness. Again, here was Jesus offering God's love and blessing to everyone irrespective of who or where they were. This 'grace', or undeserved kindness from God, is endless. It knows no limits or boundaries. It has no preferences or priorities. God's grace is constant and timeless with a beauty that defies explanation. Rather than read a library full of books about the subject, why not simply experience all that God has for us? God wants the best for us today, tomorrow and the days after that. His love for us is constant and there's nothing we can do to make us feel that we deserve it. It's a simple fact, God loves us and wants us to experience life to the max. God wants nothing but the best for us. Isn't it easier to place our trust in the creator of such a vast solar system than put our faith in what we see and understand?

Give every member of the group a candle. Light your candle and then light the candle of the person sitting next to you. They, in turn, light the candle of the person sitting next to them and so on until every candle has been lit. Ask the group to focus on the candle flame. Explain that just as one candle can light another, so can God's love be passed on to those we meet from day to day.

(Allow 5 minutes for this.)

While the group are still holding their candles, read the following prayer:

Lord,
    although I want to understand so much,
    and be able to explain everything that I learn,
    I can't help feeling that it's just not possible
    to put everything into words,
    or reduce what we see and experience
    into a formula or rule.
Some things are just awesome,
    without boundaries,
    without limits
    and are best left
    for the eye and heart to soak in their beauty.
Just as the sun shines on everyone
    without us waking up each day
    and reading a scientific textbook
    or listening to some long-winded debate
    about why and how,
    we accept the fact that it's there.
Surely that's a bit like your love for us?
We really don't need to understand
    every little detail to appreciate it:
    it's simply there,
    for me,
    for them,
    for everyone.
And I think that's totally awesome.

To the power of Three! _____

Matthew 3:13-17: The baptism of Jesus

Equipment:
paper/plastic straws
string
table tennis balls
sticky tape
pens
paper
music and lyrics

Divide the group into small teams. Give each team eight straws, sticky tape, one metre of string and a table tennis ball. The objective for each team is to build a structure which will transport the table tennis ball one metre along the string without any form of propulsion other than gravity.

The easiest solution is to build two tripods (using three straws in each!) with one tripod higher than the other. Stretch the string between the two tripods and make a carriage from the remaining two straws for the table tennis ball.

(Allow 10 minutes for this activity.)

Working as a team is never an easy thing to do. Why not have a look at: 'Holy Spirit rain down.' (*The Source 2*, 745) or 'Jesus, Jesus you are the one.' (*The Australian Worship Collection Book 2*, 55).

(Allow 5 minutes for this.)

Ask the group if they thought the lyrics developed a particular theme or idea.

Read Matthew 3:13-17.

The baptism of Jesus is a remarkable episode in the New Testament. The scene of Jesus' plunge into the waters of the River Jordan and John the Baptist's claim that it should be Jesus baptising John are often used to pinpoint the start of Jesus' introduction to the general public. However, an often overlooked part of this whole episode is the fact that it is at the River Jordan that the three characters of God are displayed. Firstly, Jesus showed everybody that the first step towards a relationship with God the Father was in repentance through baptism (water being a sign of purification). The second stage was the appearance of a dove as a sign of purity and graciousness. This vision of the Spirit of God not only confirmed Jesus' work on earth but reinforced what John had said when he told the crowds, 'I baptise you with water . . . but someone more powerful is going to come, and . . . he will baptise you with the Holy Spirit . . .' (see Matthew 3:11).

The final stage was the voice from heaven, which declared '. . . This is my own dear Son, and I am pleased with him' (verse 17). The voice of God the Father brought the whole concept of the three characters of God together. At the River Jordan, the Father, Son and Holy Spirit acted as one to announce the beginning of reconciliation between the human race and God.

Distribute the pens and paper to the group and ask them to write down what they think the characteristics and behaviour are of a Father, a Son and what they think is the role of the Holy Spirit.

(Allow 5 minutes for this.)

Put some of the group's ideas about God the Father, Son and Holy Spirit up on the wall for everyone to see. Suggest to the group that they should spend a few moments in quiet while they consider the concept of God as having three characters and as you read the following:

Lord,
> although I've no real idea
> how to understand the concept
> of you having three parts,
> I can relate to the idea
> that you know what it's like
> to have someone who
> acts as a parent,
> telling us what to do,
> when to do it,

how to do it,
and that it's for our own good
(although we really don't want to do it,
but who said anything about choice?),
and you know something about being a parent,
wondering if their child
is going to be all right.
Are they doing as they have been told?
Who are they hanging around with?
And should they really be seen
with those less than desirable people,
who everybody says
are sure to be trouble with a capital 'T'?
And you know all about that Holy Spirit bit,
the part that most people,
would rather leave in the margins
of their memories,
where it's convenient to forget
and only drag out the details
on special occasions,
like weddings, funerals
and getting Easter eggs.
Isn't this Holy Spirit thing
supposed to be just as important?
You know, it's the bit
that Jesus said would be with us
all the time,
even when we feel useless,
powerless and everything-less?
Lord,
help me to appreciate
all that you are,
everything that you can be
to me,
and every person
on this large lump of earth.

He did what?

John 2:1-11: Jesus at a wedding in Cana

Equipment:
paper and pens
small cross
music and lyrics

Prepare several sheets of paper by writing one of the sentences below at the top of each sheet.

1. I found a banana skin on the floor and . . .
2. When I woke up this morning, I yawned and . . .
3. I swallowed a marshmallow and . . .
4. I brushed my hair and . . .
5. After I finished reading my book, I rubbed my eyes and . . .
6. I washed my face and . . .
7. I started to squeeze the spot and . . .
8. I felt really sick and I . . .
9. I took the piece of cotton wool and . . .
10. I gargled the water and . . .

Distribute one sheet of paper to each member of the group. Don't let anyone show their neighbour what is written on their own piece of paper. Ask each group member to think of a response to the sentence but *don't* let them write the response on their own piece of paper. Get them to pass their sheet of paper to the person on their left. When they receive their neighbour's paper, they should write the response they thought of for their sentence on that piece of paper!

Have the group read the results aloud. Should be good for a laugh.

(Allow 5 minutes for this activity.)

Sometimes people do such amazing things and we are often left in a state of wonder.

Take a look at 'For all that you've done' by Dennis Jernigan (*The Source*, 108) or 'You are mighty' by Craig Musseau (*The Source*, 594).

(Allow approximately 5 minutes.)

It's almost impossible to be prepared to expect the unexpected. When people behave in a way which is totally different from what we expect, then we are often left feeling confused, perplexed or even disappointed.

Read John 2:1-11.

The wedding at Cana was one of those occasions which Jesus was expected to attend because the family had been invited. You can imagine the look on his face when Mary told him to go and get himself ready: 'Oh, do I have to go?'

For the two people getting married this was a major celebration. Both during the wedding ceremony and afterwards the couple would be treated like royalty. They would even be dressed in special robes and wear crowns. On such an occasion it was important for everything to go according to plan. Everything had to be done properly. It was really important not to disappoint your guests when the celebrations could last for several days. So it wasn't only the couple who were to be married that looked forward to the occasion.

In a village or town, it was almost certain that you would get an invite to attend the wedding of any family member or friend. It was accepted practice that, if you were invited to their wedding, you were obliged to return their hospitality and provide a similar quality and quantity of food and wine.

The wedding at Cana was really the first public appearance for Jesus and his disciples. The disciples must have wondered what they were doing there. Jesus had recruited them to join with him as he set about his ministry and here they were doing the social domestic bit. Not only that, but rather than show some authority or perform an outstanding miracle that would have the Romans shaking in their boots, Jesus is on the receiving end of his mother's worries about the host's wine supplies. His reaction is to ask his mother not to tell him what to do, especially not in front of the disciples! (Parents never change.)

But, rather than see the hosts embarrassed, Jesus performs a miracle that would have made the authorities laugh rather than suspect that here was the Saviour.

Jesus doesn't ask for the local newspaper to be there or demand that this miracle should be performed in front of large crowds. In fact, the guests are unaware that a miracle has happened, all they know is that the best wine has been brought out last.

Think about it. Jesus dealt with a situation that would have caused a lot of embarrassment and possible financial problems if the hosts had had to send out for more expensive wine. Jesus hasn't changed. He still wants to be with us in situations that we find difficult or in problems that are likely to cause pain.

Provide each member of the group with a piece of paper and a pen. Ask the group to think about a situation or a problem that is giving them some grief at the moment and write it on the paper. Fold the paper. Place a small cross on a table in the centre of the room and ask the group to place their piece of paper at the bottom of the cross.

(Allow 5 minutes.)

Ask the group to be quiet and to think about the problem or situation which they've written on the paper. While they are quiet, read the following:

Psalm 69:13-17.
But I pray to you, Lord.
So when the time is right, answer me
    and help me with your wonderful love.
Don't let me sink in the mud,
    but save me from my enemies
    and from the deep water.
Don't let me be swept away by a flood
    or drowned in the ocean or swallowed by death.

Answer me, Lord! You are kind and good.
Pay attention to me! You are truly merciful.
Don't turn away from me.
I am your servant, and I am in trouble.
Please hurry and help!

Walk this way!

John 1:43-51: The first followers of Jesus

Equipment:
empty can of dog food, complete with label!
small cutlery fork
two Mars bars cut into small chunks
one small cup which will fit into the can of 'dog food'
a flipchart
music and lyrics or drama sketch
paper and pens
metal tray or heat-resistant plate
matches

When the group has arrived and you are ready to begin, start to complain that you have been really busy today and haven't had time to eat since you woke up. On the way to the session you popped into a shop to buy something to eat. Unfortunately the only thing they had was a can of dog food. Well, the label said how nutritious the food was and that it kept dogs healthy, so what's good for a dog is good enough for you! Begin to eat from the can, using the fork. Chew away with a huge smile on your face, exclaiming how good the food tastes!

Ask if any of the group are hungry and would they like to try some of your food? Really encourage one or two of the group to try the 'food' and get them to agree that the food tastes good without them saying what they think the 'food' is. When you (or the group!) have had enough of the 'dog food', let everyone know that the 'food' was in fact a Mars bar.

Ask the group what thoughts went through their head as they watched you eat the 'dog food'. Why didn't some of the group accept your offer of sampling the 'food'? What made some of the group want to sample the 'food'? Why did they trust you? Write some of the responses down on the flipchart.

(Allow 10 minutes for this activity.)

Trusting in someone or something takes a lot of courage. Have a listen to 'All the way' by Rich Mullins (*The Source 2*, 625). Also take a look at 'His love is higher' by David Ruis (*The Source*, 171). Try to have a copy of the lyrics available.

(Allow approximately 5 minutes.)

Discuss the chosen piece of music. What did the group think about the lyrics? Did the lyrics have anything to say about trust and faith? What does 'faith' mean? Can the group suggest any possible meanings? Write the responses on a flipchart or A3 sheet of paper. It isn't important to find an acceptable definition of 'faith' at this moment.

Read John 1:43-51.

Jesus travelled to Galilee where he met Philip. Philip was from Bethsaida, the same town as Andrew and Peter who had travelled to Galilee with Jesus. It is quite probable that Philip knew both Andrew and Peter, who were fishermen. Jesus tells Philip, 'Come with me'. Quite a simple statement but one which Philip responds to with enthusiasm. The important point for Philip is that Jesus had gone out of his way to 'find' him and Philip puts his trust in what Jesus said. Philip goes to find Nathanael and tells him that the one Moses and the prophets wrote about is fulfilled here in Jesus of Nazareth. Nathanael's response is, 'Can anything good come out of Nazareth?' – In other words, can anything good come out of a place which was seen as a bit of a joke for a lot of Jews. Nathanael doesn't think that God would have anything to do with a fairly new town which has little heritage and no culture! He can't believe that God would have the Messiah come from somewhere like Nazareth! But when Nathanael actually meets Jesus he discovers that there is nothing outside God's control and nothing or nobody that God will not work with!

Two important points stand out from the reading:

- Firstly, it doesn't matter to God who we are or what other people think of us. God isn't interested in status or our credibility. When Jesus said, 'Come with me' he knew exactly the type of people he wanted to work with! He just wants us to trust him.
- Secondly, even though we find it difficult to believe that God would want to work with people others call 'ordinary', this doesn't limit God. We need faith in a risk-taking God!

How will we respond when Jesus goes out of his way to find us and says, 'Come with me'? How do we deal with our reactions – 'Why me?' 'I can't do that!' 'Don't you mean somebody else?' 'I haven't got the right background!' 'I would, but . . .'

Ask the group to reconsider the concepts of faith and trust.

- Can they think of other definitions?
- What do the responses of Philip and Nathanael tell us about trust and faith?

Jot some of the discussion ideas down on the flipchart.

(Allow 5 minutes for this task.)

Distribute a small piece of paper and a pen to each member of the group. Suggest that they consider their own responses to the question of faith. What obstacles stop them having faith in God? What difficulties do they have in trusting God? Ask the group to write their obstacles and difficulties on the piece of paper and fold the paper when they have finished. Collect the folded papers and place them on a metal tray or heat-resistant plate. Set light to the papers and read the following prayer as the papers go up in flames. (Alternatively, place the papers in a rubbish basket or refuse bag.)

God, it's not easy.
There seem so many things that get in the way.
It's difficult to understand,
    why you want to work with me.
I can't imagine what you have in mind
    when you say, 'Come with me'.
But you know me better than anyone,
    although there are some things I would rather you didn't know!
Even knowing all my doubts and fears,
    you still look my way.
I place all my obstacles and difficulties before you.
Deal with them.
Though they appear huge to me,
    together we can work through them.
Thank you for trusting me.
Help me to trust you.

Out of the ordinary

Luke 2:22-40: Simeon praises the Lord

Equipment:
selection of toilet rolls
squares of newspaper
music and lyrics

Ask for three or four volunteers from the group. Explain to the volunteers that they are about to take part in a consumer test which may have an amazing impact on the development of future products.

Blindfold the volunteers and sit them to one side of the room. Lay out a selection of toilet rolls on a table. The selection should contain samples from as many different brands as possible. Try to have a range of samples which varies from total luxury to sheets of cut-up newspaper.

Ask one blindfolded volunteer at a time to feel the paper and then try and identify which is the luxury paper and which is the newspaper. Repeat with the other volunteers.

When you have completed the 'test' ask the volunteers to take off their blindfolds and now repeat the test. Was it easier to identify the different papers without the blindfold? Or was it just the same with and without the blindfold?

(Allow 10 minutes for this activity.)

Most of the volunteers should have been able to identify the newspaper from the luxury paper even with the blindfold. We rely on our senses to help us appreciate and understand the world around us. But, sometimes, we may need a little more than just our senses to help us.

Have a look at 'Men of faith' by Martin Smith (*The Source*, 354) or 'I walk by faith' by Chris Falson (*The Source*, 253).

(Allow approximately 5 minutes for this.)

Ask the group how they could tell the difference between the different rolls of toilet paper.

Read Luke 2:22-40.

After the birth of a baby, Jewish tradition dictated that the mother of the child was to stay at home and not take part in any religious festivals for 40 days, if the child was a boy, or 80 days if the child was a girl. After that time the mother took part in a ceremony called 'purification after childbirth'. The mother had to go to the temple and give a lamb as a burnt offering and a young pigeon for a sin offering. The offering of a lamb was quite an expense and not everyone would have been able to afford it, so an alternative was to offer two pigeons. This was known as 'the offering of the poor'. Verse 24 of the reading states that this is precisely what Mary and Joseph did. This indicates that Jesus didn't come from a wealthy home or have all the trimmings which would have made him appear anything other than another baby from an ordinary family.

Simeon was an old man who believed that God would one day send someone who would become the 'champion' of Israel. This 'champion' would be 'Christ the Lord' (Christ meaning 'chosen' or 'anointed' and Lord meaning 'having power and authority'). So, Simeon knew that God intended to send a very special person, someone chosen by God and having God's authority to carry out God's instructions.

With these indications to go on you could easily get an idea of someone who stood out from the crowd, someone who looked and sounded different from the rest. God's Spirit tells Simeon to go to the temple and meet this 'special' person. Various images must have been going through Simeon's head as he approached the temple. Simeon was a man who studied the Bible (Old Testament) and spent time praying. He would have been aware of the prophet Micah and his writings, which said the Lord would choose someone from Bethlehem to become the 'Shepherd of Israel' who would care for his people (see Micah 5:2-5).

When Simeon got to the temple he would have been looking for a young child, but in a city the size of Jerusalem there must have been a lot of parents bringing their children to the temple. How would Simeon know where to look? How would Simeon recognise this special child? Would he have expected the child to belong to a poor family?

We're not told how Simeon eventually recognised the child Jesus. But we are told that Simeon was delighted and praised God when he took hold of the child in his arms.

Jesus lived an ordinary life in most ways and experienced the difficulties that most people felt. He was fully aware of how hard life could be and how insecure people could feel when there didn't seem to be enough money or work to provide for the family's needs. Whatever the problems or difficulties, Jesus knew about them and experienced them – and today he wants to be with us no matter what our circumstances.

Write the word 'faith' on a piece of paper and display it on the wall. Ask the group what they think the word means and, most importantly, what role does it have in their life?

Encourage the group to be honest even if that means some of the group saying that faith doesn't mean anything at all to them.

(Allow 5 minutes.)

Suggest to the group that they might like to spend a few moments thinking about faith and what it means to them as individuals. After a short while read the following prayer:

Lord,
    can I trust you?
You know, when things get hard,
    out of hand
    and just a bit messy?
Can I trust you
    when my head thumps
    from the millions of hassles
    that cloud my day?
Can I trust you
    when my eyes are tired and my brain aches
    and my feet want to give up and go home?
Can I trust you
    when I feel cold, lonely,
    unlovely, hurt and scared?
Can I trust you
    when everything I try to do
    and everything I try to say
    just make things worse?
Lord, can I trust you
    to keep me safe,
    to protect me from harm,
    to sort out the hassle and the grief?
Lord, be with me.